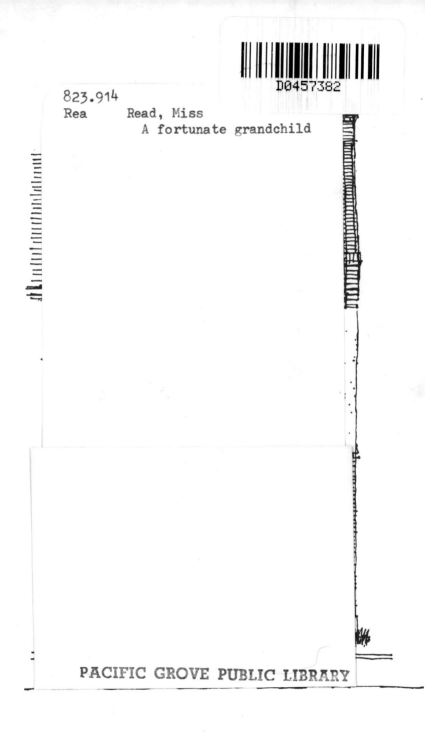

A
Fortunate
Grandchild

A
Fortunate
Grandchild
by
Miss Read

Illustrated
by
Derek Crowe

Boston
Houghton Mifflin Company
1983

First American edition 1983

Copyright © 1982 by Miss Read
Illustrations copyright © 1982 by Derek Crowe

Library of Congress Cataloging in Publication Data

Read, Miss.
A fortunate grandchild.

I. Crowe, Derek.   II. Title.
PR6069.A42F6   1983   823'.914   83-10720
ISBN 0-395-34419-0

Printed in the United States of America

V   10   9   8   7   6   5   4   3   2   1

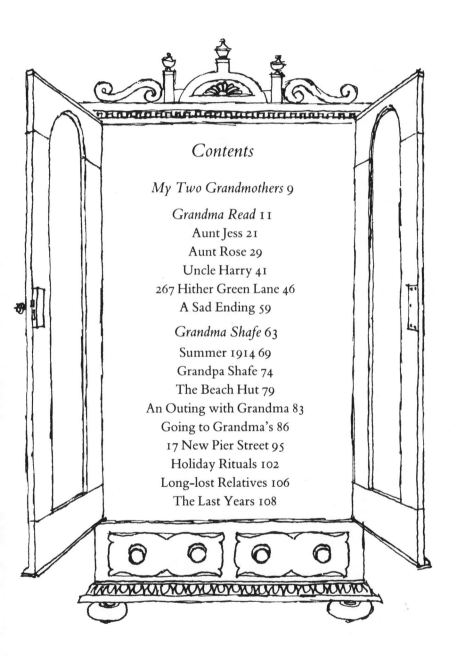

Contents

Author's Note

I am much indebted to my sister who confirmed or amended a number of these memories.

I should like to thank also my cousins Doris Shafe and Reginald Davies who supplied the photographs of our grandmothers and some happy recollections.

Most of the events recorded happened some sixty or more years ago, and I am conscious that there may be errors. For these I claim full responsibility, and hope that they may be forgiven.

To
Those Who Shared
My Two Grandmothers

My Two Grandmothers

I was lucky with my grandmothers. Both Grandma Read and Grandma Shafe were dears.

I was not so lucky with grandfathers. One had died years before I was born, and Thomas Smith Shafe was as daunting to a child as his jolly wife was welcoming.

Speaking generally, it seems to me that grandmothers have a very special place in the affections of young children. Not obliged, as parents are, to provide food, shelter, protection, advice and discipline, day in and day out, they can afford to be much more easy-going. The unexpected present, the extra outing, the little treat of a favourite meal prepared especially to delight the child and, above all, the time to listen to youthful outpourings, all make a grandmother a loved ally. It is hardly surprising that the bond between grandmother and grandchild is often stronger than that between parent and child.

My own two grandmothers were alike in the affection they so freely bestowed, and the love they inspired. They were quite different in looks, one small and dark, the other large—*very* large—with curly white hair. One had borne twelve children, the other four. Grandma Read was the widow of a Deptford builder. Grandma Shafe's husband Tom was a retired Post Office worker. More of him anon, for although he does not play a large role in this account of my two grandmothers, he nevertheless made his presence felt at 17 New Pier Street, Walton-on-Naze, where they went to live when he retired.

But it is Grandma Read of 267 Hither Green Lane, Lewisham, that I remember most vividly when I was a very young child, and I will describe her, her family and her home first.

Grandma Read

Sarah Ann Read
1846–1922

Grandma Read

S HE was my mother's mother and must have been nearly
seventy when I first became conscious of her in about
1915. At that time, my father was serving in France
with H Battery of the Royal Horse Artillery, and my
mother was carrying on his job as an insurance agent. My
elder sister and I were left with Grandma Read, who lived
nearby, for most of the day.

She was small and neat, with a very smooth skin and
dark hair parted in the middle and taken back behind her ears
into a bun. Her hair remained dark and glossy until her
death at seventy-six. It was generally believed that she had a
Portuguese forbear and her looks would certainly bear this
out.

She dressed well. Her frocks were of dark silk, usually
brown or black, trimmed with lace and made with a high
neck. She was particularly fond of prettily-trimmed bon-
nets worn tied under the chin with ribbons. As children, we
often gave her bonnet trimmings of feathers or velvet for
her birthday or Christmas presents. One particular bonnet I
remember clearly, trimmed with velvet pansies of different

colours which framed her face and delighted my admiring eye.

An older cousin of mine remembers her as 'a very happy lady. She had a nice smile, and her eyes smiled too.' That too is how I remember her.

She was a wonderful companion to young children, cheerful, spritely and not over-anxious, as so many adults are, about the niceties of correct behaviour or the awful consequences of such daring feats as jumping off low walls or down the conservatory steps. Having had twelve children of her own, she was probably past worrying over much.

She indulged me in small ways, and I loved her for it.

During that war, food supplies were extremely short, especially in London. My mother had instilled in us that we were never to ask for sweets, or anything with sugar in it because people had so little. My grandmother, however,

would frequently spread butter—or more probably margarine in those dark days—on half a slice of bread, and then scatter brown sugar on it. I watched greedily as she cut it into fingers which I soon demolished. I knew, as well as she did, that this activity was only undertaken when we were alone, and I had enough sense, even at three, to keep our secret.

Twice a week Grandma Read left her house to walk a few hundred yards to a small cinema. She adored films—black and white and silent, of course—and rarely missed one. They were changed twice a week, and Grandma returned from her outings much refreshed. Sometimes she was accompanied by one of my aunts or a cousin, but she was perfectly happy to go alone. Charlie Chaplin, Pearl White, Mary Pickford and all the rest, provided her with exciting enough company.

St Swithun's church a little farther along the road was the family's parish church. I cannot remember if my grandmother was a regular member of the congregation but my two aunts, Rose and Jess, certainly were, and clergymen,

choirboys and other church members often came back after the service to 267 Hither Green Lane for refreshments, and to sing round the piano in Grandma's drawing-room. My sister, three years older than I am, was as bored as I was on these occasions, and it was she who showed me how delightful it was to creep behind the piano, and sit there among piles of sheet music in comparative peace.

Of the twelve children born to my grandmother, eight survived, which was not a bad percentage in those days. The date of her marriage I do not know, but probably about the mid-sixties of the last century. She told her children that her wedding dress was much admired, and that she wore 'an

aerophane bonnet with gooseberries on it'. What aerophane was nobody knew, but the unintentional couplet is unforgettable. Queen Victoria was on the throne from the time of Grandma's birth until she was in her fifties. It was not a very healthy time for babies or their mothers, and I suppose that to have eight out of twelve living to maturity was not bad going.

The first child, my uncle George, I never knew. He had emigrated to Australia, married there and had children, one of whom was called Harlene. As this was also the name of a hair tonic of that time, the family found it an odd choice. I don't think Grandma heard from him very often.

My aunts Liz and Nell were married with children, and my mother, the last but one of this long family, had produced my sister Lil and me. Another sister, Betty, was born much later, in 1927.

Of the remaining boys, my Uncle Chris was married but he and my Aunt Maud were childless. The three unmarried children, my Aunt Jess, Aunt Rose and Uncle Harry, lived at home with my grandmother, so that the house was always busy and there always seemed to be someone free to take an interest in one's pleasures.

I knew all the Beatrix Potter stories before I started

school, thanks to one or other of the aunts who always seemed to be able to spare time to read them to us. They also sang to us, as did my mother (it was a great family for singing). As well as the more obvious nursery rhymes such as 'Ring-a-ring-of-roses', we rejoiced in such roistering music hall numbers as:

> Joshua, Joshua,
> Nicer than lemon squash you are!
> You'll be pleased to know
> You are my best beau!

(Naturally, I thought this had some obscure connection with my hair ribbon.)

Or, rendered at a terrific pace:

> Any old iron? Any old iron?
> Any any any old iron?
> You look sweet, just a treat,
> You look a daisy
> From your napper to your feet.

We sang too, unconscious of their poignancy, the contemporary war-time songs such as:

> Goodbye-ee, Goodbye-ee
> Wipe the tear, baby dear,
> From your eye-ee!
> It is hard to part I know,
> But I'll be tickled to death to go!

In the great cupboard under the kitchen dresser, Grandma had two wooden grooved butter pats, and these she would give me with a large lump of plasticine. Bashing happily, I tried to emulate the deft strokes of the grocer at the local Home and Colonial Stores who slapped up pounds of butter and margarine on a marble slab, ending up with beautiful striped oblongs. Mine were less symmetrical, and the din must have been prodigious, but I cannot remember anyone objecting in that indulgent household.

Another object which I admired in the kitchen was a

pin cushion in the shape of a Chinese doll. It had a round head with a pigtail, and its stuffed body was made of dark red satin. It was occasionally lifted down from its peg by the mantelpiece for me to hold, but I was not allowed to play with it in case the pins and needles, with which it bristled, scratched me. No doubt, the aunts and Grandma also envisaged me swallowing some. In any case, after a brief period of admiration, it was returned to safety.

Never did I feel that I was a nuisance, as I must have been quite often and, looking back, I realise that it was Aunt Jess who bore the brunt of my relentless attentions. She deserves a few pages to herself.

Aunt Jess

M Y Aunt Jess, the youngest of the brood, was virtually house-keeper and general dogsbody. I loved her dearly. She was small in stature, rather skinny, and had dark hair which she frizzed with hair tongs heated in the fish-tail flame of the gas bracket in the bedroom. I watched this operation with great interest. The smell of singed hair was alarming. Would my Aunt Jess go up in smoke? Nevertheless, I much admired the semi-Afro fringe which resulted.

When she took off her gold pince-nez, her eyes looked weak and as though they belonged to someone else. The look frightened me, as much as the dreadful concentrated look of my mother as she threaded a needle. Perhaps it was the complete withdrawal into another realm which shook me. I only know that I was relieved when Aunt Jess replaced her glasses, which made a cruel red indentation on each side of her slightly snub nose, and my mother succeeded in threading the needle, and both returned to me.

Aunt Jess had been trained as a dressmaker, and at the

top of the house was her small workroom. Here there were the most fascinating objects.

A large model figure encased in shiny sateen dominated the room. From the hips down was a wire cage, but above that the great swelling bust billowed out regally from the wasp waist. The whole thing was topped by a shiny wooden knob where the neck should be. Aunt Jess referred to this inanimate companion as 'Arabella', and always seemed to be hovering around her, with her mouth full of pins, as she draped material over that exuberant bust.

Aunt Jess also had the miniature clothes which she had made when she had learnt her craft. These miracles of feather-stitching, tucking, hemming, smocking and so on, were mounted on cardboard and we were not allowed to touch them. There was a long work bench, covered in black oil cloth, much scratched by scissors, pins and other tools of the trade. I remember adding to the scars by trundling an object with a little wheel up and down the surface. It left a fascinating row of pin-pricks, but a slap on the hand put a stop to this pleasant pastime.

Of course, there were drifts of tissue paper patterns, and transfers in blue print on flimsy paper depicting unlikely flowers, garlands and geometrical edgings. There was also a delicious substance called, I believe, tailor's chalk, which was flat and shiny, and used for marking material. Sometimes, Aunt Jess would give me a broken piece. If licked, it clung to one's lips rather disconcertingly. It drew beautifully though on pieces of brown paper, spread flat on the

kitchen floor, ready for my artistic efforts later in the day.

In this minute room, Aunt Jess fitted her clients' clothes. I don't know if she had many customers, but she certainly had very little time for this particular pursuit. She did most of the cooking, house-cleaning and laundry work, for I cannot remember any help in the house, and it was a fairly large one to keep clean.

She also made a good many clothes for the family, and I can remember several of the things she made for us as children. My sister and I were resplendent in black and white check coats, with black velvet collars, at one stage. I had a white muff on a cord round my neck with this rig-out. Whether Lil also sported one, I cannot recall, but if she objected, I have no doubt she was spared. She was a strong-minded child.

Aunt Jess also concocted green velvet frocks for us with curious tabs round the waist, somewhat reminiscent of mediaeval tunic decorations—a late-flowering of the pre-

Raphaelite influence, perhaps? Each tab was decorated with an embossed pink rose, and I can't think that a row of these round that portion of our anatomies, hopefully known as our waists, could have done anything for us. She also made us cream delaine pinafore frocks. I wore a pink-sprigged blouse with mine, and Lil a blue.

Much later, she made me a white voile frock for my confirmation. It had a lace insertion down the front, and lace edgings at neck and cuffs. I loathed it, and no doubt poor Aunt Jess was not thanked properly for it. I was much nicer at three than thirteen.

I can remember a splendid evening cloak she made for my mother for some forgotten function when the war was over. It was of bronze satin, lined with peach satin, and had large buttons covered with the same brown material. My Aunt Rose, who deserves, and will get, a few pages to herself, had painted each button with a little sprig of pink flowers, and the whole effect was stunning. All this work, on delicate or heavy materials, was done on Aunt Jess's

Frister-Rossman sewing machine. This
was a fine German instrument, and could
either be worked by turning a handle or
by a foot treadle.

I wonder now how Aunt Jess could have done such fine
work for her hands were always rough and chapped from
housework. The cleaning materials of some sixty odd years
ago were pretty fierce. Soda, Monkey Brand, strong yellow
soap cut in thick chunks from a long heavy bar of the stuff,
using the kitchen coal shovel to get plenty of 'purchase' on
it, hearth-stone for the door steps, and Brasso for knockers,
finger-plates and door-knobs, all took their toll on human
skin, and a little Pond's cold cream was probably all that
Aunt Jess's hard-working hands ever received. No doubt,
she was too whacked at night even to bother with that.

Looking back, I wonder that Aunt Jess never married.
It is true that she was no beauty, but many plainer women
have found husbands. She had a sweet disposition and was

unfailingly kind. When some years later, my mother was seriously ill, it was Aunt Jess who came to hold the fort. When my younger sister was born, it was again Aunt Jess who ran the house.

She never seemed to sit down and have a real rest. I used to dog her footsteps, up the interminable flights of stairs, or down into the terrifying cellar which ran beneath the hall and out under the front garden path. Near the cellar door was a small cupboard where newspapers were stored for lighting fires, together with bundles of kindling wood.

One day, close at Aunt Jess's heels, I watched her pulling out paper and wood, hurrying as usual, puffing slightly as she rushed from one job to the next, when she dropped her armful with a dreadful squeal, yelping: 'A mouse! A mouse!'

Shuddering, she fled to the kitchen. I looked into the murk of the paper cupboard, but the mouse had vanished. Disappointed, I returned to Aunt Jess.

Now, I am ashamed to say, I react with as much horror to an intruding mouse as dear Aunt Jess.

Although she was always busy, she found time to read, as I have said, such delectable works as *The Tale of Mrs Tittlemouse* and *The Tale of Benjamin Bunny* to us. And I can remember a favourite game of mine which she played with me whilst she was ironing or stirring a pot on the kitchen range.

The game was simple, called 'Shopping'. Armed with a basket, I asked my busy aunt for such things as Sunlight

soap, cocoa, a loaf of bread and other such basic necessities which were still procurable in war time. With a wave of her one free hand, she would deposit the invisible goods in my basket and I would pay her with bone counters.

The delicious climax came when I requested 'A farthing's-worth of currants'. At this, my indulgent aunt would cease her task for a minute and reach up to a high kitchen shelf where stood a row of metal canisters. From one, she shook into my fat palm a few precious currants. I handed over my counter-farthing, and the game ended in blissful nibbling.

I realise now how much Aunt Jess meant to that household at 267 Hither Green Lane. She was Grandma Read's right hand (for the other two unmarried inhabitants, Aunt Rose and Uncle Harry, were out at work), and an amazingly good aunt to the many children of the family who came to stay.

She was also my godmother as well as my aunt, and I am glad that my parents gave me my second name, Jessie, as a tribute to her.

Aunt Rose

MY Aunt Rose must have been some ten or more years older than Aunt Jess, and was quite a different kettle of fish. Grandma Read seemed to defer rather more to Aunt Rose's judgement than to Aunt Jess's.

Aunt Rose was small and dark, but plumper and decidedly more handsome than Aunt Jess. She had masses of glossy dark brown hair, always beautifully dressed, a fine complexion which she tended with *papier poudré* leaflets torn from a tiny booklet kept in her handbag, and very bright dark eyes like her mother's. She dressed well, and wore a good many brooches and beads.

She taught at Ennersdale Road School near-by and I have no doubt, knowing now something of the qualities needed to make a sound infants' teacher, that Aunt Rose was an exceptionally competent one. Her manner was motherly, but brisk and firm. Her standards of behaviour were high, and she would have brooked no laziness.

She was blessed too with those accomplish-

29

ments most needed for infant work. She was artistic and very skilled with her hands. Grandma's drawing-room had several of her water-colours on the walls, and she worked indefatigably at such ploys as pen-painting, crochet and something called, I believe, pastenella work. This latter involved painting such objects as kingfishers perched on bulrushes, or sprays of flowers, on to black velvet or satin, and then spraying them with minute glassy balls. The result was a shiny picture, and many a cushion cover, table runner, and evening bag were pressed upon reluctant recipients. My sister and I, as we grew older, deplored Aunt Rose's taste and her industry, and were particularly difficult about some velvet hair bands ornamented with roses which my mother insisted on our wearing, 'at least once', to please her older sister.

She must have found great consolation in such projects as classroom friezes, pasting pictures on screens, book jackets and making calendars, Christmas and Easter cards, paper windmills, artificial flowers and all the other endless forms of handwork undertaken in the infants' class. There must be many of her pupils who remember Aunt Rose with affection, and owe their basic grounding in handwork, reading, writing and arithmetic to her sound teaching.

She was a determined woman. Later, I heard just how tenaciously she had persisted in taking up her teaching career.

Evidently she had served several years as a pupil-teacher before deciding that she must qualify as a certificated teacher. For this she needed to take a teachers' training course. In those days, this needed money which Aunt Rose did not have. Grandma Read, although approving of Rose's ambitions, simply had no idea how to set about helping her.

With commendable courage, Aunt Rose went to an uncle of hers who was rather better off than the rest of the family, and put the problem to him. He nobly stumped up. Aunt Rose promised to repay him as soon as she had a teaching job, and before long she was a student at Brighton Training College, where I have no doubt she did extremely well.

It was Aunt Rose who took me first to school with her. This must have been in 1917 on April 16th, as I know that my fourth birthday was the next day. My clever elder sister

was already steaming ahead on the second floor of the great
L.C.C. building in 'the Big Girls'' department. I was
deposited in the babies' class, not Aunt Rose's, and given a
box of china beads to thread, whilst admiring the magnificent rocking-horse and making plans for an early ride.

My hopes were dashed by the afternoon when it was
discovered that I could read. I was wrenched from my beads
and the rocking-horse and pushed up one standard where I
had to work quite hard. Aunt Rose was delighted.

I was not.

Although Grandma Read was un-
doubtedly the head of her household,
and she was deferred to by all those in
it, I have no doubt that Aunt Rose
played a large part in its running. She
had plenty of business sense, and

would have been capable of coping with household accounts and such matters as insurance, leases, rates and other domestic and financial affairs.

I suspect, too, that her salary was a major part of the family's income, and she would see it was wisely spent. Not that she was mean. Although she dressed well, and always appeared with good shoes, handbags and hats, she was generous with her presents to her nieces and nephews, and gave us all some splendid books—interspersed, of course, with the regrettable hair bands, belts and collars of her own making—and I still use *Tales From Shakespeare* by Charles and Mary Lamb, published by Ward Lock, and ablaze with beautiful coloured plates and inscribed in Aunt Rose's hand:

To Dear Little Dora, with love.

It was a present for my ninth birthday.

As well as spending her money on books for us, both she and Aunt Jess were generous in taking us to the theatre as soon as we were old enough to enjoy it. We saw all the Aldwych farces with Tom Walls and Ralph Lynn, and Mary Brough of blessed memory, as well as *No, No, Nanette* and other light musicals which appealed to my aunts. We were also taken to a lavishly-produced version of *A Midsummer Night's Dream*, complete with a slowly-breaking dawn, gauzy fairies, Mendelssohn's music and the most ravishing costumes and sets. This was in the early 1920s,

and may have been the Max Reinhart production. It certainly impressed us.

Looking back, I can see that Aunt Rose's dominance in the household must have been irksome at times to her youngest sister, Aunt Jess. Grandma Read, I imagine, was able to ignore, or even be mildly amused by, Rose's 'bossiness'. Aunt Jess would have had to endure it rather more directly and, some years later, after Grandma Read's death, she and Uncle Harry together with an older sister Lizzie, set up house together, while Rose bought a comfortable house not far from Hither Green Lane which she converted into two very pleasant flats, one for her own use and the other to let to well-vetted tenants.

Aunt Rose was certainly the best-looking, best-dressed and probably the most intelligent of Grandma's daughters. She never married, although she had a steady admirer and they remained devoted for many years.

Her manner with men was somewhat flirtatious and affected, and my father, who was a cheerfully irreverent man, took great delight in teasing her. As we grew older, my sister and I were embarrassed by her affected ways, and

naughtily amused by the dark hints she gave about 'what might have been'.

I well remember walking home with her after seeing *The Student Prince* and remarking that it.was a pity that he married the wrong girl in the end. The hero's sense of duty—I was about ten at the time—seemed misplaced to me.

'Ah!' said Aunt Rose, sighing heavily into the darkness. 'Life Is Like That! One has to put one's duty to others before one's own pleasures.'

And then followed several remarks which might have been construed as Aunt Rose's personal renunciation of passionate love and blissful marriage, in order to maintain the household at 267. But, there again, it may just have been the aftermath of seeing *The Student Prince* late one night at the Lewisham Hippodrome.

As far as I can judge at this distance of time, she took her religion, orthodox Church of England, very seriously. She went regularly to St Swithun's church, and I have no doubt that much of her handwork went into the appreciative channels of church bazaars.

She also ran the Sunday School attached to this church, although one might have thought that she saw quite enough of young children during the rest of the week.

She organised the session admirably. Simple hymns and prayers alternated with handwork, making Moses in plasticine, for instance, to put into a carefully woven cradle and hidden among dried sticks erected in a sand tray. There was quite a bit of marching, if I remember correctly, when we put our collection money into a box, whilst we sang:

> See the farthings dropping,
> Listen as they fall

or something very similar.

The whole programme was conducted with great skill and gusto by Aunt Rose, and I think she played the piano as well.

Later, she and a friend, Miss Hetty Lee, collaborated on a useful manual for Sunday School teachers called *Little Children of the Church*, which incorporated these ideas, and gave appropriate lessons and practical work for every Sunday in the year, thus giving small children a basic understanding of the great church festivals and the pattern of the Christian year. It was in print for many years.

Aunt Rose's organising ability was also to the fore in helping to arrange the mammoth Fancy Dress Party which was held annually at Goldsmiths' College, New Cross.

I suppose it was in aid of some deserving cause. My sister and I, never great ones for pleasure *en masse*, rather dreaded these occasions when we were tricked out as shepherdesses, or nursery rhyme characters, in costumes made by my hard-pressed Aunt Jess. I  heartily loathed all my regalia on these occasions, and pined to go as a powder-puff, with a fetching little round hat trimmed with swansdown, in common with dozens of other six-year-olds, but I never attained this ambition.

The nadir of the evening, in our eyes, was the Grand Parade when we marched two by two round and round the enormous hall, surveyed by fond parents and the judges on the stage. Aunt Rose, aglow with pearls and satin, beamed proudly upon us as we passed.

The refreshments were always superb, and I rather think we were all given a present at the end of the evening.

Even so, we were jolly glad it was all over for another year.

A certain amount of entertaining was done under Grandma Read's roof, and I think Aunt Rose instigated much of it. I can remember a number of young soldiers, usually connected in some way with St Swithun's, enjoying tea there. From one, when I was three, I received my first proposal of marriage—or at least, 'an understanding'—but he was one of the many who never returned. His name was Reveley Brown, although this spelling is phonetic, as I never saw it written. Another young soldier married an older cousin.

Sometimes one or two of the clergy came to 267, and a frequent visitor was an old sailor called Maskell, who had been with Peary on his Arctic expedition early in the century. I imagine that some of Aunt Rose's teaching colleagues also visited the house, but I do not remember seeing them. No doubt I was then abed.

The journey to school, at least in the early days, always seems to have had Aunt Rose as guardian angel.

I was glad of this for several reasons. Quite often we saw 'the cats' meat man', who drove a little gig in which were numberless wooden skewers threaded with slices of cooked horse meat. He had a raucous voice to advertise his wares, and cat owners would run out with their pennies. Naturally, the cats came too when they heard the welcome cries.

I adored cats, and still do, and for some unaccountable reason I thought 'a cats' meat man' collected the cats, killed and cooked them, and loaded his wooden skewers so that he

could entice more to their brothers' gruesome feast. No doubt someone told me that the provender was horseflesh, and I had not listened or, more likely, I never confessed my awful anxieties on behalf of the trusting cats which followed the little cart. It was good to have Aunt Rose's hand to hold.

There was also a railway bridge across the road we traversed, and the rumbling of trains overhead terrified me.

It was only a matter of time, I felt sure, before one fell through the bridge and engulfed us all in horrifying chaos.

Quite a number of bombs fell in that part of London in the First World War. 'Aiming for Woolwich Arsenal,' said the know-alls. I certainly recall passing a great crater in St Swithun's churchyard after a night raid, and the piles of sandbags round the school walls to protect us from the blast. We were too young to be frightened much, but it was a comfort to have Aunt Rose's company.

She remained the lynch-pin of the family for many years. No wedding, funeral or other function was complete without Aunt Rose to the fore.

Despite her little affectations, which irritated us inordinately as we grew into our teens, she was an admirable woman, hard-working, shrewd, bountifully fond of children and interested in everything.

She long out-lived her younger sisters, and was in her eighties when she died.

Uncle Harry

M Y Uncle Harry, though resident at Grandma Read's, lived in a world of his own. I don't think that I have ever met anyone quite so dreamily abstracted as this diminutive uncle.

It was G. K. Chesterton, I think, who pointed out that absence of mind meant presence of mind elsewhere. This was so, I imagine, in Uncle Harry's case.

He was absorbed in two subjects. The Young Men's Christian Association was one, and some sect which believed that the future was foretold by the hieroglyphics on the Pyramids. The tribes of Israel also figured in this doctrine, and Uncle Harry was a dedicated believer.

His job was something to do with the news-  paper world, on the printing side. He went daily to Fleet Street, as far as I recollect to the *News of the World*. I know that one day he took us to his place of work, which was incredibly noisy but fascinating, and my sister and I were presented with miniature copies of the paper, which we treasured.

I suppose that he had some modest routine

job which he accomplished quite satisfactorily as he was never sacked, and which enabled his mind to rove happily over the two subjects dearest to his heart.

He was a tiny man with brown dreamy eyes, and an enormous walrus moustache. We hated receiving Uncle Harry's damp and fumbling kisses and did our best to dodge them, although our mischievous father inevitably prompted us to our reluctantly undertaken duty. Left alone, I don't think Uncle Harry would have noticed our presence, and

the part he played in my Grandma's house was a minor one.

However, when pressed at family parties, he was public-spirited enough to sing 'Little Annie Rooney', his one party piece, after Aunt Rose had obliged with 'Hark, Hark the Lark' in a tremulous soprano. (As girls, my sister and I mimicked Aunt Rose in action. Now, I confess, I sound exactly the same when I take to song.)

Uncle Harry wore neat dark suits, but what I found most intriguing were elastic armbands made of metal which he wore above his elbows over his shirt sleeves. I suppose it was difficult for such a little man to buy small enough shirts. The armbands were snapped off when he changed and were left on the dressing-table. Sometimes I was allowed to play with them in Uncle Harry's absence. No

doubt he had forgotten to put them on on these happy occasions.

He was a tireless worker for the local branch of the Y.M.C.A. and I remember going to a fête to raise funds for this good cause. The chief attraction to me was a wooden bust of a negro at the entrance. He was holding out a black hand on which one put a coin. Immediately, the hand came up to the widely grinning mouth and the coin was gulped down. I badgered Uncle Harry until he showed me the lever at the back which controlled this miracle. I have had a soft spot for the Y.M.C.A. ever since.

He had a small bedroom on the first floor of 267 overlooking the garden. It was very plain and neat—kept so, I have no doubt, by hardworking Aunt Jess—and the only ornament that I can remember was a china bust of a jester in cap and bells.

This little figurine was reversible. On one side the jester leant back, the silent bells shaken back from his laughing face, a picture of well-fed happiness. On the reverse side, the bells hung around a doleful face with pursed mouth and many wrinkles. I coveted this ornament, but was only allowed to hold it occasionally, and then over Uncle Harry's white counterpane 'in case it broke'.

Grandma Read, and the rest of the family, seemed to treat Uncle Harry with the tender indulgence given to a backward child. I doubt if he was ever asked to undertake any matter of responsibility, in case he forgot it. On the other hand, despite his apparent vagueness, he was no fool, and when finally he became the one man in the household which was set up with Aunt Jess and Aunt Lizzie, after Grandma's death, he probably emerged as a much more capable man than he had appeared when over-protected by his mother, Aunt Jess and Aunt Rose.

267 Hither Green Lane

IF Uncle Harry's room made little impression on a young child, apart from the china jester and the occasional bonus of Uncle Harry's elasticated armbands, the rest of the house certainly made up for it.

It was built of red bricks, and had bay windows and a slate roof. I imagine it was erected in late Victorian times, and was solidly built.

There was a small front garden in which I vaguely remember London Pride growing in a narrow border. There was also a thriving Pyracanthus shrub which climbed over the front of the house, and had masses of scarlet berries in the autumn. At my urgent request, Aunt Jess risked life and limb during this season by hanging out of the bedroom window with a pair of scissors, and cutting off branches for me, as I waited below, so that I could take them to school to adorn our classroom.

There was also a fascinating round metal lid in the front path which the coal man could lift up. He shot his sacks of coal down the chute here, and the thunderous rumbling mass fell straight into the coal cellar which ran under the hall of the house.

Access to this terrifying place was by means of a few steps down from a door immediately outside the kitchen. An enamel candlestick and a box of matches stood on a shelf just inside, and by this wavering light the cavern could be explored. There were recesses on the right-hand side which once held bottles of wine, no doubt, but I can't think that Grandma had many of those in store there.

From the front door, the hall seemed long to a child. My sister, when about six years old, used to wait in silent dread for the aunts to send her to the front door to collect the evening paper, which had been thrust through the letter-box.

She was convinced that the Kaiser himself, complete with waxed moustache and spiked helmet, was lurking behind the heavy curtains on the first landing. It was only a matter of time before he came thundering down the stairs to catch her before she regained the safety of the kitchen.

Grandma Read and the two aunts naturally had no idea of this nightly torture and when, years later, my sister confessed, they were stricken with remorse, poor dears.

The doors opened from the hall on the left. The first led into Grandma's drawing-room and the second into the dining-room directly behind it.

The drawing-room was a great favourite of mine—it had so many attractive things in it. The furniture

was upholstered in red plush and there was a matching red carpet on the floor. Iridescent conch shells stood on the marble mantelpiece, and there was a fascinating bead fire screen which was attached by a brass contraption to the mantel shelf.

The screen was composed of tiny beads depicting arum

lilies on a green background of leaves. Two
heavy gold tassels hung at each corner, and
the whole thing seemed beautiful to me.

The piano was much used, as I have
mentioned. It was an upright model, and some of Aunt
Rose's handiwork, I suspect, appeared on its top in the form
of a black satin runner embroidered with pink and red braid.
Some of her pictures adorned the walls, and in brackets on
each side of the over-mantel were tufts of dried blue statice.

A small octagonal table stood in the centre of the room,
and this was inlaid with a pattern of ivy leaves. Another
black satin mat, suitably embellished by Aunt Rose, stood
in the middle of this table on which a potted fern was
sometimes lodged.

Double doors behind the red plush sofa folded back to
give access to the dining-room. This was done at Christmas
time, or at weddings or other family occasions.

Above the double doors, flat against the wall, was a
green glass walking-stick suspended there by two ribbons. I
should like to have played with it, as well as the conch shells
and some china cherubs which sported themselves on top of
the piano (no nonsense here about having the lid open!) but I
was not allowed to handle Grandma's treasures, at least not
when her eye was upon me.

Years later, I described this room in a book called *The
Market Square*, where a prosperous Caxley ironmonger
called Bender North was to be found taking his ease, after
the shop was closed below, in his splendid drawing-room.

A gas fire warmed this room and another heated the
dining-room. Before each stood a small dish of water 'to

purify the air', I was told.

The dining-room was rather dark and was furnished with a long mahogany table surrounded by heavily-built mahogany chairs upholstered in some shiny black material which was probably American cloth. In one corner was a rather handsome piece of furniture in which was kept the best glass and china. Its name appealed to me, and I liked to hear Grandma directing Aunt Jess to bring something from

'the shiffernear'. (I have just looked up 'chiffonier' in the *Oxford Dictionary* and see that it is described as 'a movable low cupboard with a sideboard top', but I don't think that Grandma's specimen could have been moved very often as it was stuffed with heavy breakables.)

A conservatory opened out from the dining-room with a door from it into the garden. On family occasions, such as weddings, the children were settled in there at bamboo tables covered with starched linen cloths, at liberty to drop their crumbs on the tiled floor without being scolded. I remember we had fairy lights strung in there once. These were little glass jars, rather like fish-paste jars, in different colours and glowing from a small candle or night-light placed inside.

The first flight of stairs from the hall ended in two heavy dark curtains which had to be drawn aside on large brass rings to disclose a landing where Grandma's bedroom lay ahead, at the back of the house, over the kitchen and

scullery, and the lavatory and bathroom stood on the left. It was behind these curtains that my quaking sister imagined that the Kaiser lay in wait for her.

The bath was encased in wood, and so was the wash basin in the corner with its brass taps above it. It was a rather dark room and the small window was either of frosted glass or covered with that patterned oiled paper, beloved of Victorians, which ensured complete privacy.

The lavatory next door was equally gloomy and I seemed to spend an inordinate amount of time there after breakfast at my aunts' urgent promptings to '*try*, dear'. However, it was a quiet peaceful place, and I swung my short legs and let my mind drift very happily, successfully ignoring the growing agitation of my two aunts as the clock's hands crept inexorably forward and my mission proved in vain. I can never remember Grandma Read getting in the least perturbed by all this fuss. After twelve children, she had become philosophical, no doubt, about such transient things.

Grandma Read's bedroom was probably the one best known to me as it was here that I was put for my afternoon rest in pre-school, or holiday times. Here I was divested of my pinafore, frock and shoes, and tucked up under the eiderdown in just my vest, liberty bodice, chemise, knickers (edged with cotton crochet work which left a delightful pattern on one's thighs) petticoat and socks.

It was usually Aunt Jess who performed this task and before she departed downstairs I would plead with her to let me have a china ornament from the mantelpiece. It portrayed a little girl in a sprigged skirt accompanied by a dog, and I loved to take it to bed with me. As dear Aunt Jess was putty in my hands, I invariably won, and the pretty thing was given to me with many cautions about 'taking-great-care-not-to-drop-it-or-what-will-Grandma say?'

I knew better than to ask my Grandma for it on the rare

occasions when she put me to rest. She would give me her wonderful smile, a quick kiss, a brisk 'No!' and that would be that.

As soon as Aunt Jess had gone, I got out of bed, china ornament in hand, and explored the room. Grandma's dressing-table, complete with seven or eight little lace mats and a runner, called collectively a duchesse set, had such entrancing things as scent bottles, hair brushes, combs, powder jars and so on which I investigated thoroughly. There was also a cone-like object hanging by a ribbon from the mirror's knob, called a hair tidy. It was the same shape as the paper cone which the grocer whipped up from a flat

piece of thick blue paper on the counter
ready for filling with sugar from a scoop.

I usually examined the contents of
the small drawers during rest time. The
larger ones were too heavy to pull out.
The little drawers held trinkets, small
hair combs, little pots of face cream, nail scissors and the
like.

I enjoyed combing my own hair and then the fringe of
Grandma's hearth rug with her largest comb, and was
sorely tempted to undo the end of the pink or blue stitching
which bound Grandma's blankets. If you worked hard, it
was possible to make a dear little ball of pink or blue wool
when it had all unravelled, but my mother had not been
pleased when my sister and I presented her with the fruits of
our labours, and I never risked it with Grandma's blankets,
much as I should have enjoyed this innocent pastime.

The bedroom window looked out over the back garden. There was nothing much of excitement in it, although
at one stage Aunt Rose kept some hens there and, one
afternoon, a resourceful young cousin, aged two, successfully painted the run and the less-agile chickens pale blue.

The garden next door, however, was
a miracle of neatness, small clipped
box hedges surrounding the
garden beds. Here Eileen
lived, a most beautiful child
and to me 'a big girl' of about
seven. She was as immaculate
as the garden, dressed in

white, with fair ringlets and a stunning dolls' pram which she pushed happily round and round the paths. Her white buckskin boots never appeared soiled, her clothes were unsullied, she had a charming smile and pretty manners. If Eileen were there to look at, during my rest hour, my happiness was complete, and I would watch her as I sucked the china girl's head and hope that she would look up and wave to me.

The top half of Grandma's door to the landing was made of glass, and in each corner was a pane of coloured glass with an engraved star in the middle.

The top two, of course, were beyond my reach, but one ruby red pane and one dark blue in the bottom half afforded me infinite pleasure. How enthralling to see the landing wardrobe and, if the curtains were pulled back, the whole of the first flight of stairs, the hall stand and the front door, glowing redly as if about to burst into flames! Equally enjoyable, with one eye pressed to the blue pane, was the same view plunged into mysterious gloom. Often when busily experimenting with these sublime colours, Aunt Jess would appear at the foot of the stairs, red as the winter sun, or murky as an underwater mermaid, and I knew it was time to fly back to bed and pull up the eiderdown.

'Had a nice rest, darling?' she would say.

I always had.

The next floor comprised Uncle Harry's little room, a fair-sized landing, and the main bedroom, over the drawing-room, which Aunt Rose and Aunt Jess shared.

There was a large bay window from which Aunt Jess hung to cut the Pyracanthus branches for me. The walls were pink and the paintwork of a light colour, but to me the chief attraction was the gas burner which swivelled out from the wall on a brass bracket.

When lit, the flame was shaped like a fish tail, blue in the middle and flaring yellow at the edges. Aunt Jess heated her hair tongs in this and curled her fringe and various stray ends, to the accompaniment of much blue smoke and a strong smell of singeing.

The bay window looked across Hither Green Lane to the trees which surrounded a hospital, known as the Fever Hospital. I don't think I ever saw the building itself, but its trees were very pleasant to look upon over the wooden fence. The room always seemed to get a good deal of sunshine, and was probably the lightest room in that rather dark house.

Up the last flight of stairs lay Aunt Jess's workroom and, above Grandma's, a nice square bedroom which looked out over the garden.

This was the spare room, and always seemed to be in use either by older cousins, a visiting married aunt, or simply by the overflow of Aunt Jess's work which might be spread out, ready tacked for someone's fitting, either on the white counterpane or draped over the brass bedrail.

I believe there were attics above these two rooms, for I vaguely remember a trap door in the ceiling at the head of these stairs, but I was never lucky enough to explore beyond these limits. In any case, by the time one had pounded up all those stairs behind Aunt Jess, three-year-old legs were quite tired enough.

Sometimes I could persuade Aunt Jess to co-operate with me in a delightful game with the bells which still operated in every room in the house. These had a white china handle and were fixed beside the various fireplaces. By giving them a half-turn, a pleasant jangling sound could be heard in the distance. A box hung outside the kitchen door, near the door to the cellar, and here the bells rang cheerfully and indicated which room needed attention. I preferred ringing the bells, rushing from room to room, but if Aunt Jess could be prevailed upon to do this, which was not often, I was very content to study the result outside the kitchen door.

Altogether it was a fascinating house for a young child to explore, but its chief attraction, I now see as I look back, was the affection with which my sister and I were surrounded. Grandma Read, Aunt Rose, Aunt Jess and Uncle Harry were all busy people, but each of them could spare time and love for us.

A Sad Ending

WHEN the war was over my mother, never very strong, had to undergo surgery.

In 1921, we moved farther out into the country so that she would be in the healthy surroundings of the North Downs. It was a summer of extreme heat and drought, and the position of our new home on the heights gave no hint in those first glorious months of the sort of bitter cold which could be expected during the many winters we lived there.

However, my mother rallied well and began to enjoy country pursuits such as gardening, cycling and taking an active part in the local Women's Institute and the Glee Club, and later the church choir. Both she and my father sang well.

Naturally, Grandma Read, the aunts and Uncle Harry were frequent visitors. My father revelled in this new-found freedom after four years of active service and the anxiety of my mother's illness, and enjoyed entertaining.

The aunts were enthusiastic about the new home. I don't think Uncle Harry really took it in at all, but Grandma Read was not much impressed. As a Londoner, she much

preferred a landscape with figures, and on looking at the spectacular views which our windows commanded over some miles of rolling Kentish fields and woods, she shook her head sadly.

'It's all much *too green!*' she told my father, who relished the remark to the end of his days.

Grandma Read must have been around seventy-five when we moved away. She was still spry, still fond of her weekly trips to the cinema, and still blessed with beautiful dark hair.

She had enjoyed good health throughout her life, despite the large family she had borne, and she dreaded 'becoming a burden to anyone', as she put it.

Her father had lived with her until he died well on in his nineties, and perhaps the remembrance of all that had needed to be done for him accentuated her horror of being dependent upon her own children.

It was a year or so after our move that she died. I had returned from a meeting of the local Brownies one hot evening, and was surprised to see my mother looking red-eyed and tremulous.

She broke the news of Grandma's death to me, as I demolished a late tea, and although I felt vaguely sad at the thought of not seeing her again, it seemed to me that anyone as old as Grandma Read could not be expected to live much longer. My mother's grief seemed to be unnecessarily severe in the circumstances.

It was some time afterwards that I learnt that Grandma Read, after a day or two's slight indisposition, had decided that she might after all become the burden she so feared to be, and ended her life at the age of seventy-six, by taking poison.

Grandma Shafe

Alice Shafe (née Batt)
1860–1933

Grandma Shafe

My father's mother was a complete contrast in looks to Grandma Read. She was considerably taller, was fair-skinned and had a mass of fluffy white curls. She was also very large. Grandma Read probably weighed about seven stone. My guess is that Grandma Shafe probably tipped the scales at over twelve.

She dressed well, and always looked beautifully turned out despite her bulk. I don't think that I ever saw her undressed, but her corsets must have been formidable.

She favoured lighter colours than Grandma Read, and wore mainly blues, greys and purples. She had a number of toques, many with veiling over the face, and these sometimes matched the loose coats which reached her calves or ankles. The fashions beloved of the late Queen Mary, who was seven years younger, were those which my Grandma Shafe followed, and which suited her very well.

She was a jolly person with round merry eyes of grey, and a wheezy laugh which was a good deal in evidence. She was particularly fond of my father, with whom she had much in common, and he was always able to amuse her to

the point of reducing her to tears of delight as she fought for breath through her laughter.

It was a very good thing that she had a sense of humour for my Grandfather had very little and had been a repressive father, but I will say more of Thomas Smith Shafe later. Many years afterwards, when she was living with her daughter Eva, Grandma Shafe was asked why on earth she had married him. The answer was poignant.

'Well, dear, you see, I wasn't very happy at home.'

Surely this might stand as an epitaph to many unhappy marriages made when girls looked upon their weddings as the main aim in life.

Nevertheless, she was a loyal and hard-working wife to the man of her choice, and her children adored her.

She had been born Alice Batt, in 1860, I think in London, but I know little about her parents. Certainly she had admirers, and with her gaiety and cheerful disposition this was to be expected. One suitor she would have married, she said later, but her parents strongly disapproved and she obeyed them.

When, or how, she met Thomas Shafe I do not know for sure, but suspect that it was probably through the church. He was a good-looking young man, fair-haired and blue-eyed, very straight and slim. His looks probably attracted her, and his serious nature probably appealed to her parents who, no doubt, were anxious to see their lively and attractive daughter settled with a responsible man. It is possible that she still secretly mourned the young man whom she had refused, but certainly she was still young, only twenty-one, when she married Thomas Smith Shafe on Christmas Day in 1881.

They set up house in a respectable suburb in east London, possibly in Manor Park or Leytonstone where there was a good public transport service to central London.

Thomas was employed in a fairly responsible position

at the Post Office in Mount Pleasant, and travelled daily to his clerical work.

They always rented houses until retirement when they bought 17 New Pier Street at Walton-on-the-Naze in Essex, where I first remember them. Evidently, rented property suited them very well and they had plenty of choice in those days. It was the habit of my grandfather to move somewhere in the eastern suburbs every three or four years when he felt that his present abode needed redecoration. The mind boggles at the thought of so many domestic upheavals, but evidently Grandma accepted them with her customary good humour.

Thomas suffered severely from claustrophobia, as later my father did, and his family had chosen Walton-on-the-Naze as a suitable holiday centre when he and his brother and sisters were young, because there were no tunnels to negotiate from Liverpool Street Station.

Consequently, young Tom was fond of this little seaside resort, and it is not surprising that he kept up his visits to it and finally retired there in the early months of 1914.

Summer 1914

O UR first visit to the new home must have been in that fateful summer. My sister was then four years old, and I was fifteen months. It was during this stay at Walton that the frontispiece photograph of us was taken.

My sister is doing all that she has been told to do by the photographer. She has her legs crossed at the ankle, one hand supporting me, and a polite smile in evidence.

On the contrary, I am being obstinate, but it is the photographer's fault entirely as he has been trying to wrest my adored teddy from me on the grounds that he is too shabby to be recorded for posterity. What utter snobbery! As you see, I am having no truck with such a despicable

 fellow, and refuse to cross my legs at the ankle—even if I could with that figure—or smile. And teddy remains firmly in my grip.

Our clothes are worth noticing. We are wearing identical outfits of warm skirts and woollen high-necked jerseys, and very suitable summer wear

too for playing on an east-coast beach with the icy North Sea pounding a few yards away. We got to know those splendid stretches of firm sand very well, but I can never remember finding them too hot.

My father was an Army reservist, and so was called up at the outbreak of war, on August 4th, to the Royal Horse Artillery. His twenty-seventh birthday was two days later, and he was in France very soon after that.

I do not remember visiting my grandparents' new home whilst he was away at what was confusingly called 'The Front'. (There seemed to be two fronts. One overseas where my father was busy with guns and horses, and the other between our house and the gate into the road, where the path was tiled and London Pride and privet grew.)

But later in the war years, either late 1917 or early 1918, my father came home—mercifully unharmed—and was posted to St John's Wood where he was an army riding instructor.

He took us, as small children, to see the stables and the horses he adored, and I was put on the back of one of those noble beasts. I screamed blue murder until I was rescued. My father, I feel sure, was more concerned about the horse's reaction to such a ghastly noise than about my fears, but I am thankful to say that I have never had to sit on a horse since that day.

No doubt we visited my grandparents during that period, and certainly after the war it was our annual holiday place, and my main recollections of Grandma Shafe really begin when I was about six or seven years of age.

*   *   *

Unlike my Grandma Read who had a long family of twelve children, of which my mother was number eleven, Grandma Shafe had only four as far as I know, and I heard of no sad infant deaths which were such a common feature then of family life.

The first was a boy, named Frederick. He left home in his teens and eventually went to America where he married and had a son, called June—or so it is recorded in the family tree. Could he *really* be June? Or might he be Juan? Who knows? Anyway, with a Harlene on the maternal side of the family, it might well be June.

Frederick did not appear again. He and Grandpa had parted on frosty terms, I gather.

My father was christened Arthur Gunnis Shafe and was the second son, born in 1887. Grandpa Shafe who was longing for a daughter, was not very pleased, but evidently my father was a model baby and, judging by a photograph of him sitting up in a go-cart about the age of eighteen months, in a very fetching white bonnet with a huge crown and a satin bow under the chin, he was a fine boy, and already using the winning smile which made him so many friends when he was older.

A year or two later, Grandma Shafe was again expecting a baby, and this time she sincerely hoped it would be a girl for Tom's sake.

It was not. George Herbert Shafe duly appeared, and Grandpa was so disgusted that he refused to go upstairs to see the new baby. Poor Grandma! This little unwanted one grew up to be one of our favourite uncles.

At last, in 1891, Grandma produced the longed-for daughter who was christened Eva. She was a beautiful child

with the clear blue eyes of her father, and she grew into one of the handsomest women I ever met. She inherited her mother's energy and gaiety, was athletic, generous and warm-hearted. It was Eva who took on the main responsibility of looking after her parents in the last years of their lives, and lived up to Thomas's ideal of the perfect daughter he had always wanted.

There were no more children. Perhaps Grandma Shafe decided that to risk another son might be carrying things too far. Four children were quite enough responsibility.

Grandpa Shafe

PERHAPS this is the moment to have a short account of Thomas Shafe's family.

His father was William James Shafe who was born in 1827 and who married in 1851 a girl called Emma Eliza Gunnis. My father's second name was Gunnis after his grandmother's maiden name.

William and Emma had four children. A daughter, named Emma Lydia, then my grandfather Thomas. Another daughter, Ada, followed in 1858 and the youngest child, called Edward James, was born in 1861.

I was not destined to meet my great-aunts and great-uncles although they all lived to a ripe old age. The exception was Edward whom I met when he was an elderly man approaching seventy, and the circumstances were most unusual. But more of that later.

We did not meet them for the simple reason that Thomas had left home as soon as he could, and would have nothing to do with his family. Mind you, we only knew one side of the story, and the family may well have asked him to depart.

74

He was always a difficult man, and I suspect that he had been a sore trial to his sisters and brother. He was quite sure that he was always right, was narrow-mindedly religious, relishing the taboos imposed by Victorian standards so that, as children, we were never allowed to play on the beach or read anything other than the prescribed holy books allowed by Grandpa on a Sunday.

'Remember the Sabbath Day to keep it holy' was a rule he tried to live by, and very trying it was to the rest of the household. I can't remember that cooking a substantial midday Sunday dinner came within this rule. Maybe, women's work was exempt.

His sons used to point out that he should not read the Monday edition of a newspaper as men had certainly been employed in producing it on the Sabbath but, like so many obstinate people, Grandpa was able to bend the rules to suit himself.

Smoking he abhorred, and I expect he had been censorious about this as a youth. My great-uncle Edward enjoyed a cigar in his later years, I recall. No doubt brother Tom had pointed out that the downward path to hell awaited him as a smoker.

A copy of the New Testament presented to me when I was about eight years of age had a note in Grandpa's hand in the margin against the passage:

'And he that is filthy, let him be filthy still.'

'*i.e. Tobacco smokers*' wrote my grandfather.

There were other remarks of a like nature, aimed at enlightening the young mind, but that is the one which I most clearly remember.

He had also scored across the pages showing St Paul's journeys. The first journey had one line, the second two, and the third had three lines, all most beautifully ruled using a fine J nib. I think he enjoyed teaching.

His mind was clear, his diction precise, and he was fond of his grandchildren so long as they were completely obedient and quiet. But there was nothing warm and happy about him, and the strict rules of behaviour which he imposed upon himself—and tried to impose, unsuccessfully as it turned out, upon his family—gave him a wintry rectitude and a 'holier-than-thou' attitude which made him very few friends.

He was a lay preacher and spent a great deal of time in his study writing his discourses. There were hundreds of books—*Spurgeon's Sermons* figured prominently—but to my infant eyes there was not a readable one among the lot.

Not that we were encouraged to go into the study. Grandpa used it as his sanctum, and probably dozed in there as often as he studied.

This lay-preaching was not something which he had taken up on retirement. Evidently he had been interested in such things from early times, and my father used to enact a vivid imitation of Grandpa rapping on his study window, peering over the top of his spectacles, and calling out to his young sons in the garden, 'Go away, you boys! Go away!' when the ball had bounced against the window and disturbed his train of thought.

Sundays must have been particularly irksome to his young family. Years later, when my sister and I used to stay there alone as children, the heavy hand of sabbatical stricture was still in evidence.

In a drawer of his desk in the study, he kept about half a dozen paper-backed stories which he considered suitable reading for a young child on a Sunday afternoon.

Older people may remember some of these lugubrious effusions. The titles of those I remember were *Froggy's Little Brother*, *Buy Your Own Cherries* and *Christie's Old Organ*, and they dealt with sanctimonious children, usually dying of some lingering disease, who engaged in very unchildlike pursuits such as saving drunken fathers or reuniting parted parents. All were written in mawkish prose, revolting to any normal child, and simply asking to be parodied.

Luckily, my grandfather always retired again into his study after presenting us with our reading matter, and impressing upon us the need to keep it clean. He probably had a nap.

Grandma, as soon as the door was shut, relieved us of these dreadful books and substituted such welcome alternatives as a pile of *Home Chat*, a cheerful women's magazine, in which we followed the adventures of a dear little black boy called Epaminondas with considerable relish. It occurs to me that such stories would now be banned as 'racist'. All I can say is that Epaminondas did more to encourage a happy relationship between black and white children than any Race Relations Board could do.

Of course, if our parents were with us, we were spared the horrors of Grandpa's Sunday observances, and spent the day out of the house, either on the beach or in the shelter of Grandpa's beach hut.

When I think of Grandpa Shafe now, I see him, thin, clean-shaven with very blue eyes, and dressed in his every-day retirement attire of a fine grey woollen roll-neck pull-over and grey flannels to match.

He liked to stand with his back to the fire, warming his bony hands behind him. Those fingers were devastatingly strong when it came to tickling his grandchildren's ribs which he sometimes did when in an indulgent mood.

He was always spruce and immaculately clean and I think he loved us in his bleak way.

The Beach Hut

THE beach hut was a source of great pleasure to us. Originally, it had been sited half way down the cliff beside the steps which led to the beach.

The cliffs in that part of the east coast were much given to erosion. I can remember the terror which gripped me when I saw a garden on the cliff top gradually being eaten away, plants and shrubs sliding topsy-turvy down the incline. Eventually, the house itself went the same way, but luckily the people who lived in it had moved somewhere safer well before the fateful night.

After a few minor landslides it was deemed prudent to shift the beach hut, and Grandpa was lucky in securing a much better site directly on the promenade, so that we could run straight across the pavement to the lovely hard sand. This meant that we did not have to negotiate the stairs nor the muddy cliff path, all of which must have resulted in a much cleaner beach hut.

The floor was always slightly gritty from our sandy plimsolls, and there was a marvellous salty smell compounded of natural ozone and the creosote with which the exterior was painted once a year.

A long cushioned bench stood against the wall, and there were a number of deck chairs and a folding table. On the wall was a cupboard containing such useful things as a tea tin, sugar jar, cups and saucers and cutlery. There was a First-Aid tin, too.

There were also some cards with which we played Snap and Beggar-Your-Neighbour, and board games of Snakes and Ladders, Ludo and so on. I expect there were Draughts too, as Grandpa was a dab hand at this game, and thoroughly enjoyed huffing his way to swift victory.

Here we changed into our bathing clothes and emerged, shivering, to make the long walk to the sea. Unless the tide were really high, splashing exuberantly about the breakwaters, bathing at Walton meant a long trek through knee-high waves until one could submerge. My parents and grandparents considered it much safer at this stage and, blue with the cold, my sister and I obediently splashed out into the North Sea.

Sometimes we paddled instead, and this I much preferred. For one thing, we kept on our comfortable warm clothes, simply stuffing our skirts into garments called our 'paddling drawers'.

Our paddling drawers were made of sponge-cloth with pink and grey stripes, *round* us, of course. We must have looked like spinning tops. Some of our youthful fellow-paddlers had drawers made of mackintosh, which must have been far more effective.

However, we were quite happy with our own garments. What did aggrieve us was the fact that we were not allowed to have metal spades.

'So easy to cut off your toes, my dear, with those horrid sharp things,' said Grandma.

And so we were obliged to struggle on with our sissy wooden tools whilst children half our age were slicing through the lovely crisp

sand, and knocking up enormous castles in much less time.

We played cricket and tennis on those vast stretches of sandy beach, marking out the lines with our despised spades. We also played a simpler game called French Cricket which involved shielding one's legs with a tennis racket while others tried to hit them with a soft ball. The worst moments were when the attackers had closed in, and there you were, racket in trembling hand, knees knocking, whilst the hot breath of the enemy blew the sand from one's legs.

Then it was back to the shelter of the beach hut, to the kettle humming on the spirit stove and lovely sticky buns. There we would be out of the cruel wind which always seemed to blow, however halcyon the weather, straight from Russia.

An Outing With Grandma

My grandfather owned a plot of land between Walton-on-the-Naze and Frinton-on-Sea. This plot also had a hut on it, and occasionally in the summer we went for a picnic there.

My grandmother, whose bulk was impressive, could not walk a great distance, and sometimes a carriage was hired to take her to this picnic spot. I was lucky enough to accompany her one hot afternoon in the carriage which I think was called a landau, but I am not very well up in carriage lore. In any case, it was an open affair, with seating comfortably for four people, and a little flight of steps which folded up, or were let down to allow easy entry.

The seats were of leather and deliciously hot against bare thighs. No doubt I was wearing white socks and white cotton drawers edged with crochet made by Grandma herself. The crochet work was the size and shape of joined-up butter beans and left a red pattern on the back of one's thighs.

The driver sat high on a box in front, and held the reins in one hand and a whip in the other—not that it was ever used. The horse ambled along,

83

while Grandma nodded her veiled toque or lifted a gloved hand to friends as we passed.

She had with her a grey parasol of watered silk. At the end of the malacca handle was a round pink china knob, and on it was a minute scene of an unknown pier and seascape. At our feet was a basket with our picnic tea, and over all lay a snowy linen tea cloth.

The carriage stopped at the side of the road, only a few yards' walk across the field which belonged to Grandpa. Strangely enough, I remember nothing of the hut or the picnic or even of the return journey. But what is unforgettable is that short walk through the field on the edge of the cliff.

The sun blazed down upon a sea of scarlet poppies giving out their hot peppery scent from the crumpled papery petals. Lark song spilled from a vivid blue sky above—a sky that merged imperceptibly with the distant

blue sea. The air was strong and heady. The grass, brittle
and warm, soon clouded my best shoes with dust.

Grandma had put up her parasol. Behind us, the driver
carried the picnic basket. Holding my hot hand in her own
gloved one, we picked our way through the poppies to the
delights which now I have forgotten.

Later, I believe, Grandpa's plot suffered the fate of so
many cliff-top properties and slid into the hungry sea one
wild night of storm, taking with it the hut, the poppies, the
larks' nests and many memories.

Going To Grandma's

THE journey to visit our grandparents at Walton was quite an adventure.

Later, when we were the proud owners of a Ford car, complete with canvas hood and side curtains, we drove from London through Chelmsford and Colchester and arrived in time for tea. But, in the early days, we either went by train or by steamer.

I much preferred the latter, as Liverpool Street Station was my idea of hell. The noise and filth from the steam trains terrified and upset me. We used to cross a horrifying iron bridge under the grimy glass roof of the station. Below, the trains snorted and puffed out steam and smoke which eddied round one's legs, or sometimes hid one's parents from sight, causing agonising panic. Now and again, an

ear-splitting scream came from the engines, and men with black faces peered from their sides. They held shovels very often, and the red glare from the fire box heightened the satanic effect.

Once we were safely inside the

railway compartment, things became a little less fraught. Our cases were put on the rack, including my favourite made of plaited straw and secured with a strap round it.

It was interesting to see the little gardens of the East End trundling by. Some had washing all a-blow, some held a poor dog on a chain, or hutches with captive rabbits. Sometimes a lucky free cat squatted four-square on a wall or on the top of a coal bin, and sometimes small children waved to the train.

Later, as the suburbs were left behind, the flat fields of Essex spread away to the coast line.

'A penny for the one who sees the sea first!' my father would say.

And somewhere near Frinton, sure enough, the sea could be glimpsed and the penny won.

Once out of the train, the salt sea air engulfed us. We breathed it in in great gulps.

There was Grandpa, bending for a kiss. Grandma was at home, preparing a welcoming tea. My sister and I ran ahead, down the slope to New Pier Street, while behind us the grown-ups talked of such dull things as their health, the journey and the weather.

It was far better to go to Walton by sea. In those days the *Belle* Steamers used to start from Tower Bridge. There were several of these magnificent paddle steamers. There was the *Brighton Belle*, and the *Clacton Belle* and the *Southend Belle*. There may have been more *Belles*, but they are the only ones I can recall. Later, I believe, there was the *Royal Sovereign*.

They set off from Tower Bridge at eight o'clock in the morning, so that we had to make an early start whether we set off from Lewisham, or later from Chelsfield.

We travelled on the old London, South Eastern and Chatham Railway. On each side of the door was a small brass plate, like a miniature nutmeg scraper, for the use of smokers who ignited their matches on them. A heavy leather strap let down or pulled up the window, and across the bottom of the window frame ran the warning in two languages.

Do not lean out of the window
Ne pas se pencher dehors

The latter, of course, was for the poor French travellers, making for Charing Cross, who might be ignorant of the superior tongue and possibly quite used to putting their heads out of French trains.

We passed through all the familiar stations, Orpington, Chislehurst, Hither Green, New Cross and so on, with the exception of Petts Wood which, in those days, was a somewhat marshy tract with no identifying landmarks. We watched it turn from undistinguished fields to a spreading suburb over the years.

It was at London Bridge, if I remember rightly, that we got out.

Somehow, I connect Billingsgate with our approach to Tower Bridge, but it might well have been on another outing that I marvelled at the fish porters balancing towers of fish-boxes on their hard flat hats, with ribbons of grey slime dangling unheeded on each side of their red faces.

The steamer had wooden slatted seats on deck, and here we spent most of our time, though hanging over the railings watching the river water, and then the real sea, churning away beneath us was equally enthralling. There was a snug little cabin affair where one could get hot drinks, but it was advisable to give the lavatories a miss, if humanly possible, as inevitably some poor wretch would be there feeling sea-sick.

My father, who loved every minute on the steamer, insisted on taking us below to see the engines which fascinated him. As a very young man, he had spent some time training in Yarrow's, the marine engineers, who then had a shipyard on the Thames, somewhere near Greenwich, I

believe. Here he met another young fellow, Chris Read, who took him home where he was introduced to Chris's sister Grace, who later became our mother.

Father's eyes sparkled as he helped us down and ushered us along gangways between pulsing pistons, turning wheels and great thumping lumps of metal, gleaming with greeny-gold oil and smelling revolting. I think that Father would have stayed there for the whole journey if he had been alone, but family duties took him back to the deck eventually, much to our relief. .

I suppose we sometimes called at Southend Pier, which was a very long one, but it always seemed to be stranded in miles of glistening grey mud as we churned round the Thames Estuary and made northward, for the next stop, Clacton.

We had a picnic on deck and cups of tea from the little refreshment cabin to warm us up. Our faces glowed from the salt winds, and our hair was in stringy tangles which were going to be agony to comb through when we arrived.

Walton Pier was reached in the afternoon. There was a tremendous racket of engines as the ship edged towards the end of the pier, and much shouting and throwing of enormous greasy hawsers. Then the great paddle steamer nudged its way against the landing stage and the pier shuddered with the impact. Gangways were heaved into place, and unsteadily we disembarked.

Grandpa would be waiting for us, and we then mounted the pier tram and had the final exhilarating part of the long journey. It was marvellous to trundle over the heaving waves far below for over a mile and then to gain the well-known buildings on the esplanade, the turnstile, the automatic machines, and the nostalgic smell of weatherboarding, rusting cast-iron and salt spray mingled together to make a Walton welcome.

Our excitement at arriving at Grandma's back door was slightly quelled by Father reminding us to wipe our perfectly clean shoes on the door-scraper by the step.

It made us realise that, no matter how warm was Grandma's hug, nor how splendid the tea spread in readiness, it was here that we had to mind our manners, and to be extremely careful not to annoy our grandfather.

We knew of old, and had been reminded several times before our arrival, that the freedom we enjoyed at home and at Grandma Read's was somewhat restricted at 17 New Pier Street. This we accepted. It was all part and parcel of a holiday at Grandma's, and we learnt to respect the conditions which were there imposed.

17 New Pier Street

OUR first visit on arriving was to Grandma's bathroom which was upstairs.

I can still remember the lovely smell of Grandma's Erasmic Violet soap, its oval shape and beautiful purple colour, with which we washed our hands—filthy from the steamer and the tram.

Grandpa's soap was on the wooden bath rack which spanned the white bath. His, as befitted such an ascetic character, was plain Lifebuoy, and its fresh carbolic smell mingled with Grandma's Erasmic to give an unforgettable fragrance.

Next door to the bathroom was the bedroom which my sister and I shared while we were there. It was a square, sunny room over the kitchen, and looked out upon the small neat garden. Its great attraction for us was the pair of Staffordshire china dogs which stood one at each end of the mantelpiece.

The double bed was covered with

a white honeycomb bedspread which I believe was called a
marcella counterpane. They were in much favour at this
time, had a fringe at each side and were easily washed.

Our father and mother were housed along the corridor
in a bedroom which lay over my grandfather's study. It was
not as brilliantly light as our own for the one window was
partially shaded by the side of the house.

The third bedroom was at the front of the building and
was considerably larger. Here my grandparents slept, and I
remember little about its furnishings except that the general
impact was of large pieces of well-polished mahogany, and
curtains discreetly drawn two-thirds of the way across the
windows.

Below this room was the drawing-cum-dining room,
dominated by a large oil painting of a Victorian gentleman
in dark clothes. I never knew who he was, but his eyes
followed one wherever one stood in the room, which was a

little disconcerting. Perhaps he was a Shafe, or Batt, or even a Gunnis. No doubt he ended up in a saleroom, and the handsome gold frame alone should have brought in something.

The windows looked out upon the quiet side street, and Grandma frequently sat here watching the neighbours go by as she did her crocheting.

Under the stairs stood an armchair, the sort with a carpet seat and painted wooden arms which would fold up.

Upon this stood the pile of women's magazines beloved by Grandma, and among them the *Home Chats* which would provide us with mental refreshment on Sunday afternoons.

Almost opposite the chair was the door to Grandpa's study. Normally, I imagine, it would have been the household's dining-room, but here it was the place, as I have explained earlier, where Grandpa retired to write or read his theological articles, or simply took refuge from the mundane world of cooking, cleaning and the chatter of Grandma's friends.

The kitchen, which led directly into the little garden, was the real heart of the house, and had that vivid seaside luminosity which came from the great East Anglian sky.

Here Grandma cooked her splendid meals, succulent roasts, shiny brown pies, gooseberry tarts and bursting sausages.

My sister and I squeezed together on a small window-seat, my father and mother sat at each end, and Grandpa and Grandma sat in their usual places in front of the gleaming kitchen range.

My grandfather always said grace, which we had to remember, as it was unforgivable to pick up knife and fork before this little ceremony. We also had grace at the end of a meal, and I can still remember the time when my grandfather, knees bent and eyes shut, said grace whilst holding a milk jug in one hand and a plate of cake in the other.

We had had tea in the garden, sitting on the white slatted seat there, and he had begun to clear the table when

he remembered that grace had not been said.

'We thank Thee O Lord for this Thy bounty. Amen.'

We echoed the Amen. Grandpa's knees straightened, he opened his eyes, and bore the food towards the kitchen.

He was an abstemious man, never drinking anything alcoholic, of course, and occasionally singing abstainers' songs, such as:

> I like to take a social glass
> But only when it is filled with WATER
> It makes the hours so pleasantly pass
> And fills the air with laughter.

I need hardly add that this filled my irreverent father with mirth, which he was prudent enough to suppress in his father's presence. Evidently, as boys, they were given little tracts showing the evil results of strong drink. I never had the luck to see one of these, but I gather that you started in the middle with a picture showing two men. One took to drink, and he proceeded from 'The social glass' (*not* filled with water), and then to reeling home where he beat his wife and children and went later, of course, to the pawnshop where he sold all his household goods for more drink. His family ended up, ragged and thin, outside the workhouse door, and he lay in the gutter in a dreadful stupor, or else in a pauper's coffin.

The other man's family was well-dressed and in blooming health, as all its members had in their glasses was what one of my uncles called 'Corporation Pop'. This man had a large house and garden, and a bank account to match. I must say, those Victorians had the knack of putting across a message, and I only wish I could have studied it first-hand.

Grandpa Shafe also ate very sparingly, and never left anything on his plate. He polished it with a piece of dry bread until any remnants of his first course had vanished. He then turned his plate over and was ready for a slice of apple tart, or a little cheese with a dry biscuit. What happened when the pudding course was stewed fruit and custard or a sloshy sort of trifle, I can't think, but I imagine that Grandma prevailed upon him to have another plate on those occasions.

It was a very pleasant house, and I think they had chosen well for their retirement. Not only was it in Grandpa's beloved Walton and near the beach, but it was a compact well-built house which

Grandma could run easily. It was amazingly light. The woodwork and walls were lighter than in my Grandma Read's house, and the curtains were less heavy.

Looking back, and comparing the two, it seems to me that the house in Hither Green Lane was a Victorian one, and furnished in Victorian style, sombre and heavy. Grandma Shafe, some fourteen years younger than Grandma Read, was still comparatively young when Edward VII came to the throne and perhaps some of the gaiety of that era was reflected in the furnishings which appealed to her, and which she enjoyed buying when the time came for retirement in 1914.

In any case, the very atmosphere surrounding the two houses was startlingly different. The air of London was thick with the smoke of thousands of domestic, as well as industrial, chimneys. At Walton-on-the-Naze the air was clear and fresh, and sunlight was reflected from the vast sea and sands which bounded it.

No wonder we returned from our holidays in high spirits.

Holiday Rituals

THERE were certain rituals, rather like the 'Penny-for-the-one-who-sees-the-sea-first', connected with Walton.

One thing which we always did was to get up very early and accompany Father for a bracing pre-breakfast walk along the esplanade. On our way back we visited the baker's where we purchased enough hot rolls for the household's breakfast. There was a wonderful smell of fresh bread which added to the ravenous appetite already engendered by the early morning ozone.

Then there was the trip to Stone Point. This was undertaken in a rowing boat, nobly propelled by our father while Mother sat with the steering ropes over her shoulders and confused left with right. We trailed our hands, or our scorned wooden spades, helping the progress of the boat.

A picnic basket lay in the bottom, and there was always a melon for dessert. It would have been unthinkable to go to Stone Point without a melon on board.

Stone Point itself was a somewhat bleak stretch of fine sand loosely bound with marram grass. But the beach where we landed was of soft squelchy sand in which one sank up to one's knees when jumping from the boat. It was most frightening when we were really small but, as the years passed, we became quite blasé about it, and enjoyed tearing along this sea edge holding Father's hand, and roaring with laughter at the sucking sounds, the tumbles and the general exhilaration of all this exercise.

We had to keep a sharp eye open for the tide. It ebbed very quickly from this particular creek, and on one terrifying occasion the rowing boat was caught in the mud and we began to fear that we should never return to the haven of Grandma's house. The mud smelt appalling, and there were grey and black clouds piling up at sea. I rather think some more holidaymakers came to our rescue, and helped to rock and tug at our boat until we were freed. It was wonderful to

get back to New Pier Street after such an adventure, and this
time we wiped our shoes thankfully on the door-scraper.

*   *   *

Of course there were other ways of going to Stone Point or
the other places of interest on the Essex coast. One was by a
public boat, much larger, called the *Minoru*.

These excursions were announced by the Walton
Town Crier, who added considerably to the pleasure of our
holidays. We would hear his hand-bell ringing while we
were eating the hot rolls at breakfast. We all paused, cups

suspended in mid-air, rolls half-way to mouths, to listen to his booming voice:

Oyez, oyez, oyez!
This is to give notice!
The *Minoru* will make a trip,
Down the river,
Leaving the Old Water Mill
At Ten Thirty
FARES ONE AND SIX!

Then he would announce other items of interest, more excursions, articles lost and found, and generally get the attention of all his listeners.

I wonder if there is still a Town Crier in that delectable little town.

Long-lost Relatives

O NE day when we were sitting in the beach hut, my
father went for a stroll along the promenade and
met a man and his wife who spoke to him.

They were accompanied by two small boys, one about
six, the other just a toddler. The man introduced himself as
Albert Shafe and said that he believed that the families were
related.

It seemed miraculous to us as children that we should
have stumbled across these relations. In fact, it was not
really so surprising.

My grandfather and his brother Edward, my great-
uncle Ted, had been taken to Walton-on-the-Naze as children, so it was natural that the place was known to his
family although Uncle Ted actually preferred to take his
own children to such places as Herne Bay and Margate. He
may not have wished, of course, to bump into brother
Tom, who went there frequently and later, of course, lived
there.

My father and this newly-found relative, Albert Shafe,
the son of Edward Shafe, were first cousins, and had plenty
to talk about. We soon made friends with the little boys, and

the upshot was that they were all invited to visit us at Chelsfield. They so liked that area of Kent that later they bought a house quite near us, and we enjoyed their company for many years.

Uncle Albert had a magnificent voice and he and my father enjoyed singing together. This discovery of another branch of the family was of particular satisfaction to my father who was glad to feel that the breach between his father Tom and brother Ted had been partially mended in the next generation.

Later, I believe, Grandma and Grandpa met this young family at Walton, but I very much doubt if Tom and Ted ever met again.

The Last Years

IN the early thirties, Grandma Shafe, who was then just in her seventies, fell ill and went to be nursed by her only daughter, Eva, who lived at Palmers Green.

Eva had one child, a schoolboy called Reg, to whom Grandma was devoted, and it was a very happy household.

Grandpa Shafe stayed on at Walton. No doubt it seemed prudent to keep the house going in the hope that Grandma's health would improve and that she would be able to return. Unfortunately, it was not to be. She died in 1933 at the age of seventy-three.

Grandpa lived for another two years, tended to the last by Eva, the only child of his four whom he truly loved.

I look back upon my two grandmothers with deep affection and admiration.

Neither had enjoyed an easy life, and when I first became conscious of them, they had just survived one of the most appalling wars known to mankind.

Nevertheless, they were always patient, kindly and laughter-loving, and it is perhaps this last quality of facing life with humour and zest which gave both my grandmothers that aura of warm happiness which they shared so bountifully with their grandchildren.